# Join the No-Plastic Challenge!

## A First Book of Reducing Waste

**Scot Ritchie**

**Kids Can Press**

Thank you Jennifer Stokes for making this book happen — S.R.

– Acknowledgments –
Many thanks to Sarah King, Head of Oceans–Plastics campaign at
Greenpeace Canada for generously taking the time to review the manuscript.

Kids Can Press gratefully acknowledges the financial support of the Government of Ontario, through Ontario Creates; the Ontario Arts Council; the Canada Council for the Arts; and the Government of Canada for our publishing activity.

Published in Canada and the U.S. by Kids Can Press Ltd.
25 Dockside Drive, Toronto, ON  M5A 0B5

Kids Can Press is a Corus Entertainment Inc. company

www.kidscanpress.com

The artwork in this book was rendered digitally.
The text is set in Futura.

Edited by Jennifer Stokes
Designed by Katie Gray

Printed and bound in Malaysia in 3/2019 by Tien Wah Press (Pte) Ltd.

CM 19  0 9 8 7 6 5 4 3 2 1

**Library and Archives Canada Cataloguing in Publication**

Ritchie, Scot, author, illustrator
Join the no-plastic challenge! : a first book of reducing waste / written and illustrated by Scot Ritchie.

(Exploring our community ; 7)
ISBN 978-1-5253-0240-4 (hardcover)

1. Plastic scrap — Environmental aspects — Juvenile literature.  2. Plastic scrap — Juvenile literature.
3. Plastics — Environmental aspects — Juvenile literature.
4. Waste minimization — Juvenile literature.  5. Source reduction (Waste management) — Juvenile literature.  6. Refuse and refuse disposal — Juvenile literature.  I. Title.
II. Series: Ritchie, Scot.  Exploring our community ; 7.

TD798.R58 2019    j363.72'88   C2018-906066-2

# Contents

# No-Plastic Day

It's Nick's birthday, and the five friends are taking the ferry to the island for a picnic. Nick has been learning about plastic pollution, and he's given his friends a challenge: to go all day without using single-use plastics.

**Many plastic items are used only once, then thrown away. These are called single-use plastics, and they make up about half of the plastic we use every day.**

# How Plastic Is Your Home?

There are many things we can use instead of single-use plastics. Nick's mom wraps food in waxed paper and uses glass jars for storage. But there are other types of plastics that are part of our everyday lives.

**Look around your home. How much plastic do you see? Plastic takes so many shapes and textures that sometimes we don't even know we're using it.**

computer

chair

broom

flip-flops

gum

pen

phone

clock

blender

picture frames

curtains

lamp

toy

dish soap bottle

fleece jacket

suitcase

# Change Is Good!

Before they catch the ferry, Nick's mom takes the friends to a special store that sells environmentally friendly products. Some of these products can be reused, and some are made of materials that decompose, or break down naturally, leaving no waste behind.

**Stopping plastic pollution means making changes. One thing you can do is plan ahead when you go out. Bring your own water bottle and have reusable cloth bags on hand for shopping.**

Bamboo water bottles

Seaweed containers

# Plastic Planning

Everything is packed up, and it's time to go! The five friends have all brought their own water bottles and reusable bags, and Yulee even brought her own dishes and cutlery from home.

**A lot of store-bought food comes in plastic packaging, so Nick's mom baked a cake and is bringing it along in a reusable container.**

# Plastic and Animals

Sally notices that the ferry's snack bar doesn't have a recycling bin, even though they are giving out plastic containers and cutlery. Plastic that isn't disposed of properly can be dangerous to animals. They might eat the garbage and get sick.

Turtles, whales, seabirds, seals and fish have all been found with plastic in their stomachs. We can help to protect animals by not using plastic — and manufacturers can help by making less plastic in the first place.

# The Last Straw!

Max and Ollie are thirsty. Sally asks for a cup of water, then realizes it comes with a straw and lid. She says no thanks and asks to have her water bottle filled instead. Millions of straws and other single-use plastics end up in city sewers, plugging drains and stopping the flow of water.

**You probably know the three *R*s: reduce, reuse and recycle. Now there's a new one: refuse! Say no thank you if you are offered single-use plastics such as forks, cups, containers, lids and straws. But keep in mind that people with certain disabilities rely on straws for drinking.**

# Nick's No-Plastic Birthday Party

As the five friends pack up their lunch dishes, they know they've learned a lot. They've gone all day without using any single-use plastics. Now it's time for cake and fun!

**Instead of balloons, Nick and his friends have decorated with kites and streamers made of natural materials.**

# Words to Know

**biodegradable:** anything that decomposes, or breaks down naturally, with the help of bacteria or other living things

**fossil fuel:** a natural fuel, such as oil or gas, formed in the earth from plant and animal remains

**gyre:** an ocean current moving in a large circle

**manufacturer:** a person or company that makes things from raw materials

**microplastics:** plastic that has broken down into tiny pieces the size of a sesame seed or smaller

**nurdles:** small plastic beads that are melted down to make common plastic objects

**plastic:** a human-made material created from fossil fuels that can be molded into many things

**recycle:** to alter or change something so it can be made into the same or a different product. This reduces waste and limits the use of new materials. Many things can be recycled, including water bottles and plastic bags.

**single-use plastics:** plastics that are used once then thrown away